PRAISE for Becky

Becky's poetry draws you into a wonderfully complex dreamland that defies analysis and yet is perfectly logical. At times her images are gloriously tangible — eating a fig, floating in seawater, a body's smell, a touch of skin, a burnt dinner, insurance premiums. The sensual, the ephemeral, the prosaic — all of these inhabit her poetry along with gardens, nature, family, her love of Greece and of New England, her wide-world concerns, woven fearlessly together into a web as intricate as life.

I have followed her words for decades, starting from a summer afternoon so very long ago, sitting outside her stone house on the island of Kea where she first read me some of her poetry. Those early poems still resonate with me, even though, at the time, Becky had barely begun to identify herself as a poet. Through all these years I have heard her poetic voice grow in confidence, maturity and force. Each poem in this collection is a gem.

—Irene Theotokatou, actor, writer, artist, teacher, Athens, Greece

For Becky Sakellariou, all life is blessing. These poems are rich in language and meaning, deep in compassion. She takes in the world from two shores, Greece and New England, and astounds us "at every moment." Her images are sensual and passionate: peeling a pomegranate, growing a garden, the terrors of war, tributes to artists and writers, the pleasures of a lover. Becky knows "We are still human despite reports to the contrary." She knows that:

> People are hungry and lost
> but the sea still soaks up the silvered
> March sun until a whole sky
> is shining beneath the waves.

These poems are a gift I will return to again and again.

—Patricia Fargnoli, author of *Winter* and *Then, Something*,
  former Poet Laureate of New Hampshire

No Foothold in this Geography

Becky Dennison Sakellariou

Becky Dennison Sakellariou (signature)

BLUE LIGHT PRESS ◆ 1ST WORLD PUBLISHING

1ST WORLD
PUBLISHING

SAN FRANCISCO ◆ FAIRFIELD ◆ DELHI

1st World Library
PO Box 2211
Fairfield, IA 52556
www.1stworldpublishing.com

Blue Light Press
www.bluelightpress.com
Email: bluelightpress@aol.com

Book & Cover Design
Melanie Gendron
www.melaniegendron.com

Cover Art
Danis Collett

Author Photograph
Jorge Arteaga

First Edition

Library of Congress Control Number: 2017933818

ISBN 9781421837741

*This book, these words, these poems belong to
all of us who yearn to make meaning of our worlds,
to glimpse grace, to reach for the beautiful,
to be the beautiful.*

You who let yourselves feel: enter the breathing
that is more than your own.

—Part One, Sonnet IV, Rainer Maria Rilke,
Sonnets to Orpheus, translated by Joanna Macy

". . .I love[d] the wild things and the free, the things of
change and circumstance."

—Francis Ledwidge

ACKNOWLEDGEMENTS

"The Virgins of Nemea," *Guidebook*, 2011

'Back when I was still wild," *Dos Passos Review*, Fall 2011

"I will miss the strawberries," *Smoky Quartz Quarterly* (ezine), Fall 2012

"Midnight Rain," *Comstock Review* (finalist), 12/13

"Do Not Disturb," *Northern New England Review*, 2008

"The Spaces in Water," *Common Ground Review*, Spring 2007

"Directions on Picking and Eating a Fig," *Touchstone*, 2012

"Praise Song for Winter," *Northern New England Review*, 2010 and *River of Earth and Sky: Poems for the Twenty-First Century*, Anthology, Blue Light Press, Diane Frank, editor, 2015

"A Long Time the Place was Empty," *Weekly Hubris* (online) 3/19/12 and *What Shall I Cry?* Becky Dennison Sakellariou, Finishing Line Press, 2013

"Gathering," *New Millennium Writings Anthology*, 2014 (honorable mention)

"Only a Mile Further On," *What Shall I Cry?* Becky Dennison Sakellariou, Finishing Line Press, 2013

"Some Principle of Being," *What Shall I Cry?* Becky Dennison Sakellariou, Finishing Line Press, 2013

"The Blue Edge of Orange," *Northern New England Review*, 2011

"Offering," *White Pelican Review*, spring 2008

"Dream, Paused" (as "Coming Rain"), *What Shall I Cry?* Becky Dennison Sakellariou, Finishing Line Press, 2013

**Some of the above poems originally appeared in slightly different versions*

TABLE OF CONTENTS

III

• • •

IV

Of Wonder

Take a work of art to the very edge of collapse.
    —Andy Goldsworthy, Scottish artist

I

Build a spider's web,
    found sticks, narrow, knotted,
coiled and pinned together.
Weave them through each other,
    hang it from a carob tree.

Wait for it to collapse,
    first separate, then crumble in slow
motion, gathering into irrelevant
design on the frozen ground
blackened from the fire
    of an unknown earth.

Sing only
    of astonishment,
despair, wonder
    at your own life

II

which could be a hungry one,
    a story that looks
    for emptiness on snow,
    swans frozen in a lake,

a kidney stone, caramel-colored, smooth
    and layered like an onion,
    never seen before by the urologists —
She will probably die if they attempt to remove it.

What color was it really? will you paint it?
    will you dig a cave for it in the snow field?
will it disappear into the ribcage of the whale
    you did not build?

Whatever you do will sink.
And the woodcocks will return
    in the month of the Full Worm Moon
    and eat their weight in worms.

III

Carve a hole in the river
Watch it become a deer
Notice the deer turning
toward her fawn

Release the hole
To song and threads
Carry the colors
Until they wash into steel

Find the point of collapse
Go to the other side

Seven Stages of the Decomposition of a Piano
(and thirty-two keys)

notes of honey and pine nuts
almond and hazelnut
you braid my hair under the oak tree

the great human-headed Syrian lion
winged spirit of stone and Helios rising
straight from the ocean
the imagined still underwater

Jesus knew
that dangerous place
those awful consequences

but still he sang
I am poured out like water
over the Rain Shadow side of the mountain
so full

This is all we have
the quiet light of aspens
the outline of a soul
the world in shadows he said
a stretched universe of red

the silence of moving silvered water

the opening sky
swallowing
our eyes into unfathomed distance
blinded into white

Conception II

The complete stillness of the first 24 hours after conception

the pause before creation
no time
no breath held   no breathing
no bloody heartbeat   no body mass
no echoes   no sound

only a liquid stillness
two ideas   one folded into the other
before entanglement   becomes being
becomes the passage
the twisted coils of future identity

       • • •

Step into that starlight,
leave behind the psalms,
thermal pollution,
your mother's face,

lay them in a row along the edges of the exhausted earth,
all that you have ever known,

slip off your casings, your skin,
your gathered margin-notes,
capture a white, moist soul,

lift it high
break it like an egg
into your heart
sing its infinity

The Virgins of Nemea

Before the sun caught
the brief dew of night, before the sea
went black and silver,
the young girls of Nemea
picked sheaves of pungent wild *selino,*
then wove them into crowns
for young athletes.

The earth's smells, hot
inside their nostrils, carried them
to the young men's gleaming bodies.
Heads bowed, they laid the wreaths
in other men's palms,
elders who knew how
to handle smooth golden skin.

Light burned
into black auburn,
their red-stained feet
broke through a landscape roped
into dark gold furrows, cradled deep
in the memory of their births.

A man digging in the broken Temple of Zeus
stops his work, lifts his head
in the white Peloponnesian sun,
then moves toward the near field
where grapes grow into wine
that tastes of pepper and plums.

He bends between the vines, gathers
armfuls of blood red poppies,
returns, scatters them

among the hard orange
earthen graves lined with pale bones.
He knows they are the bones
of young girls.

Later, the girls walked
into a sea stained lavender.
Fecund, open, their singlets
plastered to their curving skin,
they bore the beginning
of a woman's shame
to show her desire.
They knew, then, only their own bodies
and what they must not want.

Forget Your Perfect Offering

      —Leonard Cohen

for there is none.

When we learn this one final story,
we will walk on our hands,
let our skirts slide over our heads,

not worry if anyone sees
our underpants,
our skinny upside-down thighs.

Later we will fly to Kyrgyzstan,
ride long-haired black ponies across the blustery steppes,
our heads wrapped in camel skins,
sour goat's milk in horn-shaped leather pouches.

After Kyrgyzstan, we will visit Uzbekistan,
eat roasted red peppers stuffed with white cheese,
flat bread fried in oil,

slathered with onions and baked *fava* beans,
later, sweet stewed grapes
sprinkled with almond slivers.

We will completely *forget our perfect offering*
because it will always have been perfect,

perfection being just the way the light
seeps through the cracks
in the curved goat-skin roof.

Crossing

After an installment by Kalliope Lemos, 2006

Every year, thousands of desperate Iraqis, Somalis, Pakistanis, Kurds and Afghanis walk hundreds of kilometers overland to reach the western coast of Turkey where they hope to find a boat in which to cross over to Greece. The boats are wooden, old and leaking. The traffickers often travel in speedboats alongside the migrants until they reach Greek waters. They then try to sink the boats so that the Greek Coast Guard will pick up the migrants as they are required to do by law. If they are picked up in the water, they cannot be returned to Turkey. Many of them drown and many are rescued.

I found the boats rotting,
scattered across the night beaches of Inoussa.
Twenty-six of them, hollow
of human form, abandoned to the darkening sand,
the wind, the salt.
Their occupants had fled to the hills, terror
in their mouths, their children
swaddled across their bellies,
shaken to silence, always thirsty.
Oh mother my home
I cannot see you as we wake
in the morning   comfort
my skin with your hands   how
will I know
when to stop remembering

A woman in black sees them,
shouts, they crouch
in unknown grasses that smell
of trees, sounds pierce
their skin, thorns
fill the sand beneath their feet.
They lie speechless, their tongues forced
to know nothing, their throats

to swallow hard bread soaked in salt and oil.
Oh God please
take me, my baby
I bleed, my skirts pulled up
through my legs, the smell of the fish
stashed between the curved wooden planks,
their scales like lightning on the blue

I will gather these ships split
into halves, broken
by fear and a long sea, built
by men who knew
the darkness of the other moon.
I will lift them into a temple
of voices thrown across nations,
a cathedral to the aching
spirit, yellow deserts of running
human shadows, outlines against the night
sky, despair and hope
spliced through the ribs, one breath
rising hard after the other.

Dedicated to:
Jaleb b. 1979
Mohammed b. 1979
Kaea b. 1978
Ibrahim b. 1969
Motha b. 1981
Firas b. 1990
Hassen b. 1982
Ali b. 1982
Said b. 1986
Bahar b. 1977
Damba b. 1965
Habib b. 1976
Hossein b. 1986

Wassim b. 1979
Mozde b. 1996
Amor b. 1986
Bahim b. 1984
Moutapha b. 1981
Adel b. 1986
Ahmed b. 1988
Sarah b. 1987
Goulan b. 1980
and hundred and hundreds more

A Photograph Accompanies the Tao

The spider's web trips me, sound
       sinks into silk

threads, ladders stretch toward unruled
       triangles, slender shadows

quake through light particles seen
       in brief passing, zebra lotus, five crows

watching a silent bricked path,
       warnings ready at their reflections.

A girl knows the Latin name of each blossom,
       each fragile bud, stem, striation,

she opens the book to sighs of color, leaves
       that droop, drift through their own outlines,

transparent as eyelids set in water, water
       vanishing into the sky, veins

remaining on sand, diagrams of time,
       mind, sunshine.

Blood Secret

After viewing Fernando Botero's paintings
of Abu Ghraib

I thought I was grieving something
I had once touched,
a body, perhaps,
buried deep under damp soil, wrapped
in mango leaves, weighted
by stones. Or a letter never sent
in the rush of going to war,
or even humiliation in the eyes of God

as when the soldier planted his thick boots
on each side of the man's head, pale stained fingers
unbuckling his belt, cracking open
the fly buttons, pointing his fat penis
at the man's face, pissing, grinning.

I might hear from you, my teacher,
that is enough, no more of this,
but I will not stop the words
until the continent rises up,
until you who cringes sees, you
whose eyes refuse to know
the black bones and mauled dogs
eaten in His name.

You will bleed your fear
until we are nothing but sinew
laid out in the desert
without mercy.

The Ledge of the Universe

I dreamt I was sitting
on the ledge of the universe,
swinging my legs, feet in green socks
and pink ballet slippers.
Phil Ochs stood in the ocean, still.

The earth below grew dark, the snow
turned to moss, then rust.
Starlight got chopped into electronic bits,
then scooped into the invisible bowl
of a concave mirror.

Promiscuous electrons coupled
with every bum that passed by,
and the *unmoved mover* spoke
about memory and sorrow
and how our *breath increases space.*

When I awoke, I wanted to return
to the great golden, pockmarked, prehistoric wings
that opened to the north wind,
that lifted me toward snow geese and hooded crows,
that never let me down.

I could still see the universe stretching
into red, its oldest form. I heard
the silver-gray silence that suspends itself
between conception and the first heartbeat,
shifting, undetected.

Requiem for the Lost

after Auschwitz

Bones bend, fracture,
stomachs heave their hungered emptiness,
bodies, frozen, hold us upright.
We walk hard, calculated halls,
obscenely linear roads,
rooms distended, stuffed
with spirit bones that cannot leave
their place of death.

We dream through these bones
to a far sea of shifting sand
where we bathe them,
lay them out across the purple desert,
sacred graves released to the sun,
to prayer, hope and an open sky.

A noctilucent light of clouds
will shine through all darkness,
gathering around the bones,
their shapes, their shadows lined
above the scorched river beds,
no thirst, no more beating wings.

The Spaces in Water

after the tsunami

The sea unfurled onto the sand, every pouch
filled with a thousand fish
ripped from their fathomed worlds, flipping into
the white air, pouring out
over the flat wet earth.

The children rushed,
screaming with glee,
into the shallows to gather
up the fish, scooping the shiny bodies
into their wet shirts,
how pleased their mothers will be.

Their mothers seeing
the next sea moving in like God's arm,
flew through the strange water alive
with leaping bodies, calling
their children back, children spread
over the wettening sand like fresh greens
on a cloth, mothers reaching
their children, grabbing them, the water reaching
the mothers with the children in arms, rolling them
like kindling swept under and over and out.

The fathers, inland,
at work,
could not see,
deaf to the sounds,
never knew
about the fish.

What War Can Do

MH17

outside of Grabova
the bodies
lie in wheat fields
crushing large sunflowers

white flags fly from poles
placed beside each body
so they can be counted
outside of Grabova

The sky opened up
acres of deep purple blossoms
rupturing   splitting
forever gone   from blue
specks of yellow chamomile
enormous nodding sunflowers

the noise a shaking   a shivering of the still
unharvested air blowing dust pollen   small leaves
a long whirlwind into places they had never before landed

then shapes of human bodies
falling   tumbling through the turquoise summer air
like fish that had suddenly leapt out of their pools
they fell through the blue
as if God had shooed them
out of their quiet beds   outside of Grabova
a tsunami of air   *it just happened*
landing   covering the fields with disturbance
as if without bones to hold them together
yet they were *mostly intact*

All people stood still
as if they were the bodies themselves
other people rushed in   still others would not let them near
but the sun was black and burning   they did not want to wait
they begged   *please please let us take them home*
the bent and broken wheat sheaves marked with flags
broken through the tall grass   the lavender   the small daisy heads
each human being   each one
lying crooked   broken legs askew   not there

I should have finished that letter

the last slice of watermelon in the frig will go moldy

I forgot to tell her my

why didn't I

I left my

my red hat

I can't wait for

for the rest of my life

Red embroidered stockings   straw hats with ribbons
a carved cane the head a serpent   a green bandana
one woman all in black except for the blood
on her face

A gray-scarved woman bends over
searching among the wheat sheaves   gathers
small white flower heads
for winter tea
the sky above her bursting into indigo

sudden midnight lignite
purple without end or shame
an exploded plum slashing the blue
a violent midday sunset

The woman does nothing
watches as the sky fills
with tumbling silver and black
objects carrying the sunlight with them
draped across the mirroring plates
pierced with uncountable tiny holes
frozen fragments flags of white and green
she understands nothing
bends then straightens
then afraid moves quickly
toward her village   Grabova

sunflowers
a field of debris
disturbance
lavender
a black baseball hat
a sandal
the straps of a backpack

Only a Mile Further On

Late afternoon sunbeams bend
    around my feet, my eyes
infatuated by their light.

The sky curves down
    across my back, my skin
blazes with anticipation,
    my palm against my neck
    watching for the fall.

Last April, a yellow-bellied sapsucker
    was sighted at Jemima Pond
in Eastham, Massachusetts.
    I wasn't there for this fragment
    of grace. I was pushing instead

through thick-stalked, thigh-high grasses
    between my house and the quince trees,
aching with the redemption of beauty,
    wanting the final answers,
    not the problems.

You'd think there might be an edge,
    jagged and abrupt,
so you keep walking
    into that blueing distance, expecting
    only a mile or so further on

to where gray catbirds, razorbills
    and ruddy turnstones
appear across the pond
    in the late afternoon, sheltering
    shards of light

that press into the water's rough surface
    as if to pass daylight
into darkness
    through their fanned wing bones.

Lifting Through Yellow

Frozen snow circles the edge of the bowl
of the great black chasm
raw untraveled bitumen

A lament of cypress trees lines the road
a wake of the darkest green
my life unravels

I will fill with rain and sand
my heart running open with faces

and we will meet in the center where the wind
circles our legs like the dog
herding us back home

The late afternoon sunlight
rains onto the sea's dark surface
minute explosions of luminous disbelief

A dried peach pit huddles
among the smoother stones
a family eating on the beach in July

Pale gray porous rock
tiny mollusk shells nestled in holes
riven by eons of ceaseless waves

I go to that place
where I can gather the clouds in my arms
lifting through the yellow-green farmed fields
oleanders of killing pink

She wrote: *did you hear the thrush*
singing in the aspen tree
between the phrases of your poems
and the harsh guitar stokes of death?

October

I was alone in the sea today.
No elderly people in white hats
bobbing in the shallows
talking about their grandchildren
and what they will cook tonight.

They didn't come
because it had been windy last night.

I lay in the sea, nothing
in my way, nothing
in the long view of my eyes, a horizon
that held no fear
and I thought about a poem
that began: *I was alone in the sea this morning.*

The white plastic beach chairs, empty,
are lined up like boned dinosaurs
waiting to be called into the sea
to be reconstituted.

The ring that slid off my finger
as I fought the waves and lifting pebbles,
silver with pale blue abalone fragments
set along its curve, craved the water
which licked my finger and took it
into its eternal round.

I spent hours searching the beach
and the shallows for it
the next morning and the next.

The *meltemi* dried my wet, slimy skin.
I stood, letting the wind cover me, cool.
The heat blew up the last tiny blossoms
from the coral plant that dips
toward the slow western sun.

The figs coat the ground
and the almonds blacken in their shells.
No one will be here to harvest them
or tell wild tales.

The house will remain cool and silent
until the May sun pushes through
the slats of the pale green shutters,
and the dust begins to glint.

No Foothold in this Geography

I know I wrote you
that I could never love this land
      its black shadows
      that rake through betrayal and disorder.

Nothing like my passion for thick slow rain
coating heavy-leaved trees
      that block the sun
and draw solitary shadows
on the mud-soaked ground.

But when the brazen rosemary
spreads her arms across my flagstone path
      flagrantly ignoring
the meticulous zigzag designs
between olive and almond I laid out
with such intention eight years ago,

when the wasps build lines of tiny nests,
      semi-detached row houses
on the inside edges of my precarious black plastic fish pond
sunk in the earth beneath the bitter orange tree,

it is not really love but a wild, untamed wrath
that pulls the reddened skin of my chest
      into its heat,
its ruthless, merciless splendor,

that informs me   *come*
      or leave
but never again dare
to plant yourself in untasted soil

The Closest Roots

The jasmine is thirsty
I water it once in a while
it is too far away
from the rest of the garden

I have to crash
through low-hanging thick fig branches
wild onions and an overgrown vineyard
to reach the bushes

then the hose will sway and stretch
and sway some more
through the air
just to reach the closest roots

We are having a heat wave
Mozart's Requiem on my tape deck

Dies Irae   *Lachrymose*
over and over
No wonder it is thirsty
I am thirsty

for your sharp sour skin
that tastes of the cut limes
you have been known to rub
on your arms
the smell at the side of your nose

once I stood there all night

I will have to cross snow-covered mountains
in July   a salted ocean
to quench my thirst

I would bring you lavender
and rosemary
hang them in your kitchen

stand there waiting for your smells
to uncover me

Midnight Rain

The gardener smiled in his sleep.
   I woke, thinking it was the mice in the ceiling playing tag
as stone blind as they are, night as black as ever.

But it was rain, delicious, sweet rain,
   wetting our long-hard packed earth, the new persimmon tree,
the old roses, the daisies beginning to fold into themselves.

I got up, slipping to the door, barefoot
   and stood on the threshold in thrall with the sky, the water, the world,
the return of summer night thunderstorms

when we would curl up in our parents' laps
   on the screened porch, awakened by the crash and shattering echoes,
our pajamas slightly damp, the smell

of the rain rising from the earth it had just entered, counting the silence
   between the great cracks, taking in
the surprise of the world and how it astounds us every moment,

how it becomes wet when it is dry, when
   it is dark before it is light, how it holds
our lives between its poles, tipping at an angle
   that we will never truly want to understand.

When the Figs Go

Eat as many figs as possible
in the month of August.

Stuff them in your mouth
while walking or cooking,

the texture on the back
of your tongue unrivaled.

Summer is still here
as long as the seeds

stick in your teeth.
By the end of August

all that remains
are pale sacks slit

open by the heat,
bored into by flies,

flopping onto the ground
under the gray branches.

But when the figs go,
the grapes come,
and later, the olives

and so we are comforted
by the plainsong

of what is going
and what is coming,

a call to   *all is well*
   all is

Directions on How to Pick and Eat a Fig

on a hot August day somewhere
near the Aegean Sea.

First you have to be doing something else,
carting weeds off to the brush pile, holding
the dog down to pick off the burrs, thinking about
an old lover, eating bits of last night's vegetables,
standing in the brief shade.

Then it has to be about four in the afternoon,
the cicadas in their fullest chorus, biting, incessant,
when it is so hot, so bright no other person would be
where you are, doing what you are doing.

Then you can step across the dried grass cut
in May, now so hard, brittle, you cannot go barefoot,
past the new lemon seedling, the old nectarine tree,
toward the great thick, gray umbrella-wide
branches, the space beneath drawing you under it,
looking up into the fat fingered leaves, the pale
green fruit hanging in twos and threes from each joint,
scrotum-like. Some have split wide open already,
some shriveled yellow, bruised,
some still firm.

Then you must reach up and touch each one, ever so
gently pressing the skin's surface to feel which
is ready to come off, which one wants to open out
with the softest *flop*, which one will come willingly
to your fingers.

Then when you have the fig in your hand, hold it lightly,
turn it right side up, the nipple pointing to the sky, join
the tips of your thumb and fingers of each hand
and place them on either side of the fig, right beneath
the nipple. Pull the sides gently away from each other,
letting it open out, one half in each palm, the deep red
tangled seed-filled pulp ready, yes, for your lips, yes,

your mouth, your tongue, slowly, this
is what you have wanted all day,
this final slow ecstasy.

The Way My Garden Is

The quince tree asks for nothing
except for the occasional snip
of a new shoot on her lower trunk
or a yellowing leaf among the heavy fruit.
She is pleased to give me jam
and thick paste with almonds
every autumn as the air cools.

The fig tree is completely out of control,
her thick branches bending
all the way to the ground,
bowing to her own unknown gods,
taking over the east end of the vineyard,
heavy with her special brand of eroticism,
strong and durable.

I pick a fat, sun-filled fig
as I water the wilting jasmine
which seems
to survive this incessant heat
despite the droop.
If I weren't here, she would still blanket
the back fence with delicate new shoots
pointing straight to the sky
as if calling on the gods to *bring it on.*

The olive and the almond live in their own worlds.
I could be a fly for all they care.
They produce, expand, thrive and endure.
I am just here for the ride.

Whereas not the oleander, ah, yes
the beautiful poisonous oleander.
I rarely water them anymore,
they stay put in their careful rows,
expanding like great dense Vs every year.
Sometimes we prune them, sometimes not.
I like to leave the dead leaves
underneath their branches
as if all they needed
was to feed on their own flesh.

• • •

Poured Out

How we hold ourselves in,
how we release small slices, measured,
how we contain silent homes of self
that never see light.

I am poured out like water.
Sing the Psalms,
let loose the cry,
the wait of the Rain Shadow,

that other side of the mountain
where the water flows.
I am poured out
and we wait

like my grandfathers
both wood carvers
who barely knew each other,
one making tiny, intricate model boats

with gunwales, hatches and rudders,
the other full sized row-boats,
hulls painted green, smoothed
and polished-edged oars.

Their bows sluiced through
waves either imagined
or in the Lost River Gorge,
once more *poured out.*

I climb into the belly of the whale,
curl against the cartilage,
listen to his huge heart
sweeping us through the currents,

a path through the night sea,
moon or not,
red-pocked and rimmed,
a lightening horizon.

We stand vigil
over the loggerhead turtle
who died entangled in fishermen's nets,
confused, blinded, strangled.

Unstring My Bones*

"I can see. . . into next week's trees. . ." —Mary Oliver

Her white, veined hands reach
through tomorrow
like a baby smiling toward faith
a world most tender

as if she were sure
of the wounded white heron returning
to the salt marsh

the great white winged fish
in the sky
at dawn

why we need
the otter and snake
the bleached clamshells trapped
in the black bog

the steaming murky bracken
the golden lichen

she understands
that the yellow warblers will wait
for her

lifting their beaks to the spilling light
saving a place

on the narrow branch
of trembling pear blossoms

together they will gather
each soul

sing high harmonies
and fly their bodies north

*lines in italics from Mary Oliver's poem "Gravel" in *The Leaf and the Cloud*

Still Waters

On the Day of the Dead,
Joe and I toasted the many people in our lives
who have passed, naming them one by one,
a sip of Pinot Grigio for each.
It went on for quite a while.
He leadeth me beside still waters,
He restoreth my soul.

The last of our neighbors
from the days of Edmunds Road died two weeks ago,
and I cannot stop seeing the leggy forsythia bushes,
the dried goldenrod, the crows
traveling in threes across the long winter sky.
Most swallows are "ground feeders,"
preferring seeds to be scattered on the ground
rather than in bird feeders.

Today the fallen leaves, rust and faded cinnamon,
blanket the forest floor, soggy and pungent,
unhurried in their metamorphosis into black earth.
An occasional naked blackberry bramble bush
has knit the tops of its twisted branches
through the rambling sumac trees,
and the white spire of the new Blessed Mercy Church
slowly blazes red as the sun sets
just behind the new rising moon.

The wind has already been harvested.

Geese and Angels

The woman next door died last night.
          Someone opened her windows,
sparrows chattered on the dusty sills
pecking at stale seeds.

The geese flew south this morning.
          They honked with abandon
above the great spruce
but no one waited
          at her closed door.

A crow stood by the side of the road
          unruffled by the *whoosh*
of cars, the staring human eyes
or a man's imagination.

Autumn butterflies feather through
          the last of the clover blossoms
before the coming hurricane
sweeps in.

It may be that a gathering of angels
          is hovering nearby,
that they will fly with the geese,
their great white wings cradling my neighbor

on her way toward dawn.
No one will sing her psalms tonight.

Some Principle of Being*

For Stanley Kunitz

Come, quiet on your feet,
the path is lined with lavender
and yellow sweet pea.

Lean
over a bud, slip your third finger under it,
stroke it with your thumb.

Examine the folds, the shell, the possibilities
of beauty and loneliness
and of you, still here.

You know that you are going.
Your voice cradles the lilac buds,
lifting their eyes one by one.

Words are no longer written
on this grass, broken and
bent from your feet, and mine;

wild yellow mustard
takes over the field beyond, no shame,
just a tiny bitter leaf.

And a wind bends the blossom
toward the impossible
blue sides of leaves.

You have known light
and color, the teal of the clippers,
the thin rust of dead leaves

keeping the earth musty
for the unlikely event
of another season,

the silver white mica
of the moon that opens
the cavern of all our bodies.

*from "The Layers" by Stanley Kunitz

Writing the Cardinal

I cannot write
the cardinal
in the midst
of this snow storm
that blurs
all definitions,
horizon and trees.

He sits alone
in the sumac bush,
grand, cocky
and splendidly scarlet,
utterly oblivious
of the other birds,
gray, crouched,
heads bent low, waiting
out the blizzard like stones.

He is the sudden crimson of creation,
the primal brushstroke of color
carelessly feathering this morning
and my desire.

The Cardinal Again

From the dull light
between the edges of the curtains
I knew it had snowed once more,

a mid-March snow that gets everyone around here
groaning, wishing they lived
in Greece or Florida.

But no matter how cold the early air
and thick the gray skies,
I wanted the cardinal
who arrives when the light
is so low and flat
that only he is real.

I wanted him to pleasure my eyes,
to force that intake of breath
that happens with the beautiful.

He does not come to the feeder
to join the pudgy juncos
who, like popovers,
chiggle and *chivvey* on the surface
of the new snow, cleaning up
the fallen seeds, happy and unnoticed.
He will come later.

I may catch sight of him
through the small frost-misted panes
of the kitchen window.

Praise Song for Winter

Somewhere on this persistent earth
it is at last winter again
time to stand quieter than a month ago
watch the snow's steep descent
whorls of silver streaks sifting
across the glass of the north-facing windows

At last no baking heat no
insistent sun to run from
instead collars up scarves tight
iced knives of cold
slicing circles into your cheeks
keeping the windshield sticky
with frost and rime
hoarfrost now there's a word
that makes the blood run fast

It's a blessing that now
the windows can stay locked
the lamps turned on early
sweeping the amber-shaded rooms
and you imagining roots and bulbs
suspended in their season
bedded under the snow

You know that the ice will come at last
and cover the land
breaking our eyes
with a startling majesty
light prisms shattering branches
looped double to the ground
frozen grasses snapping
sculpted into spidery nets
a glory closer to God's own light
than we could ever have imagined

The Blue Edge of Orange

Along side indigo waters
of an early New England spring,
I stop the car, slip
into the cold shadowed water,
an otter diving into the murky silver.

My eyes catch the edges
of blue as I enter an object
through glistening orange membranes.

I plunge toward a place of dreaming,
cannot see if the ice below
has broken up, imagine
silky green ropes snaking
toward whispering fish
immobile at the bottom.

My wind is measured
by the crested wavelets
on inland waters, by the weeds
that pass between my legs.
Numbers spin
in the five tones
of the planetal scale,
tallying the spiraling orbits,
their wings beating constant death.

The Speed Limit

I come back to this place
of remembrance
this dark damp soil
because I need to stay within the speed limit
to be on time

I come back to be showered and astounded
by a sky unashamed by color
to gigantic oak trees that have decided
to change from the green of daily loving
to the orange and scarlet of sudden fireworks
without our permission

I come back to wet streets
the *psssss* of the tires
and windshield wipers spitting rain
to puddles and socks

and to thick forests
whose trees stand as close together
as families with long-held secrets
we can only guess at

my eyes are witnesses
the images inhabiting the inside
lining of the lids for eons
until a sign comes and the morning light
strokes its gentle breath
across the window

III

Relative Ecology Toward the End of the Week

I took the car out three times today
believing I was going somewhere essential,
somewhere qualified as important
to justify the gasoline consumption,
my carbon footprint.

I considered the environment.
I did.
And still, I went out
just forgot,
one more thing, a short hop,
just down the street.

Later, I lost a long oval wooden earring in Ivy's car
probably at the moment her year-old dog
leapt into the front seat, gouging my thigh
with her nails. Streaks of black and blue,
raw to the touch. My chiropractor was horrified.

On Friday, I lost my Vietnamese beaded bracelet
in the hospital changing room where I put on
one of those impossible "johnnies,"
walking around in my socks as if I had dementia.
Afterwards, I stuffed all the clothes into the labeled bin.
The bracelet, tiny embroidered squares of red felt
surrounded by green and silver beads,
must have gone in, too.

The best part of all was talking to Mrs. Hoang
at the Manchester Social Security office
about my Medicare Plan A: "you were never
eligible for non-totalization benefits," she told me.
"You have to pay the whole thing."

I looked at the papers, documents and notes
strewn all over the couch and coffee table,
and said, *Hell, I am going out again.*

"Pushing a sofa up Mt. Everest."

—From a dream by Mary Norbert Korte, poet, Mendocino, California

While waiting for the chicken to boil
so I can put in the rice,
so I can eat this special soup/and/tea meal,
so I can drink the awful Botania Phosphates
that will empty my insides out
so I can be ready for my colonoscopy
at nine tomorrow morning,
I found myself pushing a sofa
up Mt. Everest.
Or, at least, I thought I did.
It may have been the class system
that I was pushing against
or a terrible sadness about women
still furious with men, men
still confused about women.
Or maybe it was my daughter-in-law
who has closed her heart to me
or just the god-damned cost of living.

I don't know Mendocino
where the poet had this dream,
having been to California only once
in 1991 when my sister got married
for the third time. The boys, with their thick
black pony tails, flew in from Cleveland
singing loud Greek songs
about mothers and sons
in the back seat of the rented Honda.
Peter refused to wear a tie
to the ceremony, although he danced
with my 79-year-old aunt Elizabeth
with the right amount of measured abandon
for a twenty-year-old.

I was speechless flying over Los Angeles,
so many little square houses,
orange roofs, busy automobiles,
so many straight roads
going to and from each other.
I didn't want to go there ever again.
I called Diane to ask
if I had to fly to LA
in order to get to her.
She comforted me with color
and light and a madrigal
on her cello, probably in A minor.
Like the wind at Force 4,
a moderate breeze raising dust,
loose paper and small branches.

I think of Diane when I stand
at my ceiling-high bedroom windows,
of thin branches on lemon trees
that vibrate faintly
like her bow.

January 13, 5:28 pm

The digital clock on the stove top
suddenly went backwards,
continuing all day until it reached 00.00,
the end of the world, the prophets might say.

I burned the sweet potato and cauliflower curry
I was cooking for my weekly potluck
because every time I looked at the clock
it wasn't time to take the pot off the burner.
Everyone said the taste was unusual.
I didn't tell them they were eating
food cooked after the end of time.

Earlier I had watched velvet colors stroke the peaks
of the mountain, the pink of my very first lipstick.
Tomorrow, I will ski alongside Alan,
an autistic 14-year old
who goes straight down the hill yelling *hello*
and *goodbye* in Spanish and Greek.

When I drove through Dublin at 20 mph,
I passed words hand-chalked on a blackboard
hanging from the side of the lamp post:
  Mary Healy died peacefully in her Sleep last night.
  Services will be held this afternoon at 4
  In the Congregational Church.

We are still human despite reports to the contrary.

Back when I was still wild

Back when I was still wild,
my father never told us tales of mermaids
like other fathers, or lost islands of Mesolonghi,
only stories of duty, honor, the right thing to do.

I climbed trees in a torn cotton pinafore
meticulously smocked by my grandmother
in threads of lilac, butter yellow, sky blue,
colors meant to tame wild little girls.

Back when I never combed my hair,
sweet nettles twisting through the tangles,
my sisters and I would lean like a fugue
out over the curve of the great oak banister
hushed by my father's lecture,
his voice streaking past my unruly head,
slapping against the dark, glassed-in portraits
of stern ancestors, upright citizens
hung in a relentless row up the staircase.

Back when I went around with my hair in braids,
two woven ropes of smooth flax
lying softly against each shoulder,
boys seemed to like me more than they do now.
Perhaps it was the braids and how they must have wanted
to stroke them or maybe it was the way I stood,
one foot perched on top of the arch of the other.

Sammy said he fell in love with me
that long-shadowed September afternoon
when he saw me balanced like a mermaid,
my head tipped back, the heat and the nettles
briny like seaweed, the nearby roses,
creamy white like my young arms, their scent,
the face powder his mother carried in her purse.

I believed everything he told me,
not those others who asked for things
I was never quite sure of.
Then he, too, slipped away
like the nettles, the trace of rose,
my braids, my father's voice.

Frisbees and Hula Hoops

In the University Library Reading Room,
we recite poems about dying leaves,
dying sexuality, dying hope,
a memorial to a beloved poet
dead of lung cancer.

As the phrases fill the spaces
between our warming bodies,
I dream myself outside the library
windows, the air warmer and bluer
than on this gusty March day,

back to when I too once lolled
in the grass on the quad
under the grand oak trees,

the boys nearby studiously
ignoring our long, smooth legs
not yet stroked by the slow fingers
that we learned about later,
not even imagining the feeling

and the receiving that it takes
and how to wait through it.
As we waited through
our own brilliance

taking uppers throughout the nights
before our papers were due,
something wild-eyed ripped through
our bodies, lifting our brains

to a scale we suspected we could reach,
the trees still bare, hula hoops
and Frisbees, baseballs and the early days

of women discovering something
terrifying and alluring moving toward us
that we wanted with such longing,
no homework, title or author.

Do Not Disturb

She said, *do not disturb your father.*
He said, *you're a loose cannon.*
The neighbor said, *stop making waves.*
They all said, *no more back talk, young lady.*

My body, skinny, grew seven inches
in one year, sharp-edged elbows and knees,
ashamed, humped over to hide
my new breasts. No idea how to be.

My sisters, too, were confused.
We flopped together in the back seat
of the cream-of-tomato-soup-colored Pontiac
whispering dirty stories about vaginas

and periods, fannies and French kissing
while my father ground his teeth
and my mother cheerfully chattered on.
She had them, too: the *keep-the-lid-on,*

if-you-can't-say-something-nice,
don't-say-anything-at-all, all those instructions,
an orgy of commands on how to be and how to be *not*
that poured over our sweet blond heads,

relentless, hypnotic, as fixed as the huge oak tree
that possessed the front lawn, the one we climbed
and swung from, the one whose bark
we always touched before heading to the barn,

the hay chutes, the scary rag pile in the back stall,
the rope we shinnied up, spun down, our ankles
bloody, shrieking, falling into heaps of giggles.
We knew nothing then of the battles

to come, our lean bodies so hopeful,
so ready to be everything, anything,
to *disturb the whole universe*
just as we were meant to do.

Many Bodies

I have become my younger sister
She walks the rivers all day
      spinning the currents

My brother dreams himself
to the tops of mountains
      no heartache up there

My other sister knows moose
and Canadian geese
      surrounds herself with snow

Many bodies are contained in this one
    rows of shimmering ancestors
       genes that do not lie
even when only one heart is open

we do not forget
we dream what we do not want to know
    forgiveness enters as we lie silently
in snow   /hot desert sand   /deep green grasses
     unflinching about love

December 9, 2009

On my sister's 62nd birthday
she is still silent,
abdicating her siblinghood,
her ties sliced like a grapefruit,
the harsh juice shriveling
whatever tissues inside the mouth
might have once been pulsing.

I picture her face as I do my own,
smell her body heat,
hear her vowels.
There is no road to her home,
the chains up across the entrance,
the restraining order written loud
in four languages.

The snow on my meadow this morning
is the same snow that covers her roof,
her gardens, her leaping dogs.
I could call her and ask:
How is the snow?
What are you doing today?
Are you plowed out yet?
I would tell her that
I made egg-lemon chicken soup,
cranberry corn bread, then spilled birdfeed
all over the living room floor.
God willing, I would tell her,
happy birthday, sweetie.

Later it was the snow
that pulled me into the heavy silence
of forced closure, the nest, the fire,
the embryo of comfort.

• • •

Mary Oliver Teaches Me about Death

Tell me   tell
me
how it will be
when death
carts me off to the bottomlands.

How will I recognize them?
what colors are they?
what will happen   *when I begin*
the long work of rising...

where do we rise to?
how will I know when I have arrived?
I am afraid.

Death that slow swim   draw me
the diagram,
the street signs we will not follow,
the clothes we will not take,
the language we will not speak.
How do I say goodbye to everything?

You seem to know something about this.
You have pulled it from the seaweed,
the cattails, the *pale turnip.*

It has shown itself in   *forever/is coming,*
the turtle with her cat's head,
the pale green moths
trembling around the lit lamp,
plum-colored, storm-heavy clouds.

For what should I be grateful?
for you, your searching words, your dazzling spirit?
for the rain as it slithers across my window?
for summer corn and melting butter,
for the spicy smell of crushed olives?

Do not leave me behind
when you go.

All italicized lines are from Mary Oliver's poem, "Gravel" in
The Leaf and the Cloud

Comfort Me

I saw a language on a back road
lying hushed in a rain ditch.
I took it into my mouth
and it taught my tongue
to gather rolls and lisps, my throat
to shape ripples and gasps,
then release them like petals into the bright air.
How speaking these words would draw
me into long years gone, cradle me
through wars, invasion, hunger, rape,
every tragedy, every lullaby, every shame,
a whole new world curled under my tongue.

I stop by the fishmonger at the Wednesday street market
from whom I never buy fish.
He always tells me I look like a movie star.
I bow gracefully, receiving his smile.
I buy jewellery these days when money is short,
earrings and bangles from the Bulgarian woman
who wishes me good health.
I am comforted with silvery string,
brass clasps, knotted leather, tiny turquoise beads.

I go home, eat chickpea soup, a salad
with tomatoes and curled cucumbers.
I inspect the tiny brown olives I bought,
half a kilo wrapped in a plastic bag
with a quick knot at the neck.
I think back to Michali who talks about Obama
and honey from orange blossoms,
to Yianni, his greying moustache,
wilted arugula, leggy leeks, miniature cabbages,
his wife, cancer, not long now.

How could I not understand
the oceans of wild mustard,
their yellow pollen coating my legs?
Or the big shaggy brown bears
who migrate across the Great Ignatia Way
not knowing that it is now a concrete killing ground
of milk trucks, Mercedes, gleaming motorcycles?

How can I not understand
the cyclamen that comes up no matter what?
Or the erotic scents in the second half of August?
Or the women sweeping the streets before the Resurrection?
Olive trees moving up the hill like notes on a pentagram?
The dreams of pomegranates?

And how the earth turns,
waiting for seed?
And for rain?

The American Abroad

> "The summer mornings begin inch by inch
> while we sleep, and walk with us later
> as long-legged beauty through
> the dirty streets."
> —Jack Gilbert, "Horses at Midnight Without a Moon"

Jack knew how to sleep late
in a small Greek village
on a small Greek island,
the American Poet using
the dirt and beauty
as idols with which to examine
his fragile Self.

His was the generation
of disgruntled westerners
who believed that the simplicity
and poverty of remote rural lands
would provide The Answer. To something.
They sought to imbibe the spirits
that had forged an extraordinary nation
so they might feel whole again.
Or feel something.

But Jack could never know
hunger, invasion, eleven generations
of Turkish occupation,
Germans executing whole villages.
He did not lose his children
to the *pedomazema*
when, after a bloody, heart-breaking
civil war, the Communist Army gathered
hundreds of children from the northern borders
and sent them to Russia.

He did not know of *katohi*
when flour and water soup
with a little oil drizzled on top
was the staple meal.
Nor did he ever harvest almonds,
roll out sheet after sheet of *filo,*
dye his clothes black
in the big iron pot in the back yard
after losing his mother.

He never knew about whooping cough,
endless days and nights
without a vaccine, much less a doctor,
scared of choking in the cold, wet dark.
He did not ever have to struggle
to get the big, ornery mule
back into the stable,
nor were his hands permanently stained black
from sorting, washing and slicing olives.

What did he ever know
of rules that could never be changed?
What did he know of not having a choice?
Did he ever enter a church,
light a candle, kiss the icon?
Did he ever go to his knees
and beg deliverance from his Saint?

Pieces of an Unwritten Story

The man who gave me his window seat
on the flight from Warsaw to Athens
had gray hair cut close to his skull

but I could tell he wasn't as old as me
from the veins and tendons
in his arms when he rolled up his sleeves.

They were slightly tanned and
lightly covered with silvery-blond hair
and, although he had a serious face,

I overheard him quietly smiling
with his wife on the phone.
I would like to have stroked those arms

during the flight,
but since then I have listened to Palestrina's Masses & Motets
during my surgery

and later, when the operation took longer than expected,
some Greek love songs.
I do not remember them.

I crave some deep bodied rumbling
that will not come.
I am still bereaved.

Between warm nut bread and cherry jam
at breakfast in the B&B before leaving for the airport,
we met two Inuit women

from the northern provinces of Canada
who had come to Warsaw to perform throat singing
at a music festival

and a young male nurse from Cleveland
whose goal was to visit
every concentration camp site in Europe

because his girlfriend was Jewish.
He told us that bicycling
around Berlin was the best way

to understand that city.
We did not have bicycles
the day we were there.

English Lesson

"Countries have borders. Stories do not."

My name *Shakila. I miss clothes.*
I have just these.

My name is *Batool. I miss love.*
I want to go to Paris.

My name *Mazoum. I miss my father*
my mother are dead.

My name is *Shima. I miss my personality.*
I am no one here, no one.

My women talk in class.
They know I know no Farsi
yet they still talk.

Here they can speak
what they don't speak
during their days of crouching over a pot of greens,
scrubbing underwear in a bucket,
showering in a blue UNHCR stall.

Just behind them the desert,
border guards, an ocean
that cannot flow backward,

a broken door, sand in the *hijab,*
grandmothers at the well,
the midwife, some guns.

They cannot go home, ever again.
We have eaten the rain.
Their eyes are tired.

They do not care about CAT, COW, HOT.
They want to go where language means life,
where there may be snow and green trees,
where HAT, FAT and BLUE
will mean, simply, liberty.

Time is all over the place

the clocks go back tonight
or is it forward

they tell us to remember

how can we call
my brother in Arizona

they don't change their clocks
in Arizona
so how do we find him

my mother-in-law snorted at
daylight savings

when it came to Greece
served dinner at the "old hour"

went to bed when she wanted
never changed her elderly one-legged clock

and dismissed us when we told her
this is the way it is now

She said *this is my way*
no one will tell me what time it is

I know what time the chickens
need to eat

when they go inside to lay their eggs

when to collect ground snails
in the wet fields after a day of rain

when to check how fat and juicy
the grapes have become

nothing to do with the clock
take your clock and shove it

even the mules don't care
they know when it is time to turn toward home

when it is time to nap with one hoof
delicately raised

even the dark meadows know when
to wake us with dew-covered daisies

slithering through the blue dawn

Waiting for the Peach Blossoms

My lover dreams of Nancy Pelosi
handing out diplomas and bags of cocaine
to important people from the audience.

He believes this to be a prophesy of chaos,
a relative term, of course,
but I know what he means.

An awful war is raging somewhere
yet poppies are beginning
to sprinkle the fields.

People are hungry and lost
but the sea still soaks up the silvered
March sun until a whole sky
is shining beneath the waves.

Ficus benjamina, the Weeping Fig,
leans in lament at the vacant alter
reminding us

that peach blossoms will never bloom
although we tell you
we are waiting   /but
we do not tell you

that peach trees do not grow
in this endless desert,
the blistering sand that breeds
only bare feet running,
running anywhere   /else

As Long As I Can Come Home

from Crete this time
Ottoman throat ornaments   *makam*
glide and slither through my vocal chords
stretched like taffy

throw the notes out
high pitched like Neapolitan women
bawling to each other across swaying laundry lines
make them echo

I learn that altos
have longer vocal chords
than sopranos
and that throat vibrations
some silky
practiced on one note only
need years to perfect
some smoky   /warm them up to each other

make your voice like a river
Ahmed tells me
wail in and out
be the woman in Persia
in Byzantium

All day the composer
followed the candy-seller on his rounds
through the narrow streets
transposing the intricate modulations of his cries
into written cadence
to become the *Dugah*
a seventeenth-century Ottoman classic

As long as I can come home
drop my bags
on the floor of the entry
wipe mud and sand
from my shoes
carry the bits
of my life with me
tuck them in with other bits
building narrative
the obituary   /I cannot stop

deep sultry quavers
each flat containing at least
three internal flats
before the next note swoops over
to land seamlessly
on the smooth round top
below

then slips down underneath it
into another minor   /then

I will be home

A Long Time the Place Was Empty

—from "Little Horse" by W. S. Merwin, The Carrier of Ladders

Tonight here with you,
the place where my hand
might rest between your ribs
collapses slightly as you curl
up to sleep.
The skin folds softly,
no muscles tight or thick
in the hollow made for my fist.

We no longer speak
of the future.
The clothes of forty-two seasons
overflow the closets, lean
on each other for comfort,
a little worried about time
and age and the possibility
of our arms never again slipping
into a sleeve or a silk lining
stroking our hot skin.

And still, each peach leaf
bends in on itself, cradling
the last drop of moisture,
then, the light sliding away,
it enters the night, uncurling.

Dream, Paused

My fingers stiffen, no sun
can warm them.
I no longer lift discarded promises
from remote, dusty roadsides,
place them in a bowl of curiosity.
I cannot repeat the refrain of water.

Like the grapes. Scheduled to ripen
in late August, we waited through September,
it was odd weather anyway.
But they stayed green, no juice,
shriveling slowly
on their skinny stems.

A friend says that poetry
is *for those who know how to dream.*
Dreaming is a dictionary,
the entrance to mystery.
When will I walk through those echoes again?

He sits as still as the quince tree
on a mid-August day,
his hands forgotten on the table.
His wife has just died,
he can no longer tell
which side of his body belongs to him.
He waits for the rain to come.

My human heart wraps itself
around love, around rain,
there is no more blood, no beat.

Stripped Bodies

The leaves that fall
just before autumn
warn of wildness.
Apple tree arms
lean in stiff salutes, blood
the mirror cannot see, sits
on your body.

When you stripped
our bodies, took back
what you had given,
I saw a massacre of legless men,
boys with black guns
frantically running,
the unimaginable.

My sister in Idaho
says I wear
my heart on my sleeve.
Unbeating, it weaves
through the purple
of rust and black of worms,
worn five years for mothers,
ten years for husbands,
forever for abandonment.

The stiff blackened pods
of the Judas tree
hang like dried socks
or unpicked cucumbers
despite the north
wind that reels through
the land. You

would have loved it here:
how did you bury
all the secrets
learned at my side,
frost them over the cake
of courageous cowardice?
They all said
how brave

except your daughter
who saw you weeping,
the photographs
spilled over the cold blankets
like the first time
we played Slap Jack and you saw
who I might be.

Sorrow's House

stands in deep darkness lit only by an old dream
a recent death written across your face
or it could be my sadness caught in the walls   the dog
yowls when we drive away   your head

will not rest on my shoulder for you
would weep all night   you sleep instead
my hands in your hair   waking over and over

the red buds of the oak and maple
just opening   the horizon a slow purple
halo around the paling green of new pine
as we walk down the mountain

you cannot listen   the litany
of your thoughts   the incessant ache
inside the membranes of your grief   my words
incidental   *I am so sorry*   your hands
will not even close around mine

someone walks across the hall   you recognize
your son   your beautiful dead son
whose face alone
I already love
how can you   how can I

a blond woman in a black coat
walks crying across the bridge   crosses the traffic
as we drive underneath   we cannot know
what just happened to her heart   or anyone's

I will miss the strawberries

I will miss the strawberries,
the bending, heat on our backs,
red-stained fingers, bending, ecstatic sweetness
on the tongue,
bending, filling baskets.

And the fourth graders reading
The Declaration of Independence in the town square
We hold these truths

And then the raspberries, harder to pick than the strawberries.
You have to really want them, Rosalie tells us,
soft, falling off their buds into your fingers,
the fuzz liquefying as soon as your lips touch them.

And the balloon festival, children open-mouthed,
the sun in their hair, on their heads, in their eyes,
holding someone's hand tightly, wishing to fly,
such wonder, even desire, at blue and yellow flight,
long sky and shapes.

The roast beef supper at church, the strawberry shortcake,
the fiddles and banjos around the newly painted gazebo —
salmon and turquoise with fish and birds around the inside walls —
(*in case of rain inside the Vestry*),
people spread on blankets, tablecloths, *oh there is Joan,*
so glad she is here, and who is that
with her? Her son, Andrew? How tall he has become.

And then the blueberries. I would go like Sal did,
picking, bending, eating, clinking in buckets,
bells around our necks, maybe even a bear
and her cub, mountains of blue fruit,

enough to bring home for breakfast, pies,
ice cream, even fistfuls whenever we open the refrigerator.

And the cupcake auction with the *Hot Mustard* Bluegrass Band,
later, of course, a blueberry bash to plunge into, dark mystery
of cream, teeth, chin, throat, slightly sour from the heat,
going home slowly afterwards

where your breath waits,
the sudden pull against my neck,
my skin moving against your tongue.

Mangoes and Limes

You teach me about mangoes,
how to slice them,
the pale yellow wedge on the flat of the knife
slides gently onto the tongue,
the last flesh attached to the long pit
for licking and sucking.
I wonder if you know that mangoes are a symbol for love in India.

You are a man with roots in dry, hot southern soil,
you read the fine print in the *Farmer's Almanac*:
fogs in February mean frosts in May.
Tides, sunsets, sunrise, equinox, you know them all.
This is the way you have fallen in love with this land.

But I do not forget your limes, piles of small, hard, round
green fruit in your old ragged basket,
a drink of them — quartered including the skins,
sugar and water noisily ground up
in the blender for a good ten minutes,
frothy and slightly sour, cool and heady,
something to lean toward in thirst, to savor,
to sit and feel nothing else.
I don't know about love with limes,
but there's something about their skin, your skin, mine.

Later, you teach me a slow dance with no steps
where time *does not fly, just holds us in its arms.*
Where *knowing is not the only truth,*
like your deliberate fingers on my back, my neck,
opening my lips, weaving a single note,
unnamed, including this.

come with me tonight

come to me one more time
come fall into my body
embed yourself in me
hand in your name
your palms will become earth

craft a cave for us
the soft glow of glory and death
love the other heartbreak
the last moments of our lives

we stand behind each other
I adorn myself with you
you look at me
looking at you
as you always saw me
see me as you

we cannot move the one body
away from the other
you have become what you love
this is how we will be taken

No Sky

I heard about *harmonic convergence*
on NPR last night and wondered
if I had missed this phenomenon
while looking at your profile

while you watched
the blood-red afternoon mountainside
come closer

your hands
cupping the stories
of rancid and discolored leaves
layered around sink holes

the sinuous skin of your wrists
shaping and gathering
the velvety mushrooms
of your childhood forests

I look at you
crouched beside a fallen tree
studying the ripped bark
the torn ligaments

a wild turkey startled
by your murmurs
flaps through the birches
wings detouring toward a wild sky

perhaps this *is* harmonic
convergence although it feels
broken   /spliced
because you will tell me
that you no longer want me here

in this heart space we shared
we breathed in   *feathered* hope

Gathering

I scour the rust-red stains off my fingers,
scrub the torn nails, the blackened creases,
the heady odour of mashed olives
rising from the steam, the washbowl,
all day the gathering of the last of the olive crop
into nets, baskets, sacks.

Then you come into the bathroom
with your dark, smooth skin,
your short, strong legs, your cigarette,
and you move against my back,
press your nose into the long bones of my neck,
your moustache feathering the faintly blueing skin.
Your arms slide under my dampening breasts,
circle my waist, your hands,
square bowls of talking fingers,
enter the water, join mine,
the soap thickening, coating our skin
until there is no difference between you and me,
the olives forgotten in the spitting rain outside the window,
your skin entering mine, the smell ~
memories of when I didn't know
how to contain this rising high, the startled breath,
how to lean back into a man's moist chest,
how to give in to anything, to all of it,
to scoop myself out of myself,
to let every stitch loose, to take the fall,
the musk of work, sweat, body curves,
that ancient desire resurrected.

You will enter without warning,
my body will wash through yours,
my hair binding your mouth,

the thick, tangled, curly mass
of briny earth, rotting, matted leaves:
you, your steam, your measured stillness,
your timed indifference.

On a Marriage

no finished puzzle to put away in the box
pieces lost or stolen or swallowed but never
completed as we might have dreamed

ribbons of legs thrown over bellies
invitations for sex   /doubt   /madness
children listening from another room

watching for the expression as he enters
the kitchen   /waiting for the word
or is it she who wants to chew him up

sweet skin lost in floods of duty
words once said over and over
no longer fit the face   /the hand

that once brought hundreds
to their sides in envy   /in ecstasy
how beautiful they are

ornaments on the ear
beer and toenail polish
every possible item of a life

thrown unsorted onto the bed
unshelved   /untamed
counting on the fingers

doesn't calculate   /only the abacus
of night sweats and brushing teeth
every morning after breakfast   /or before

how could we have   /*what was I thinking*
the priest's strange words   /holy water
jasmine   /the bellybutton distended

lift the right breast out of the blouse
let it hang like a swollen white key
that cannot unlock anything

a crap-shoot   /discarded underwear
bread and oil

Reading Neruda in the Car

What will I miss?

Reading Neruda's *One Hundred Love Sonnets*
in stumbling Spanish, the syllables pausing
on my lips:
recorro tu pequno infinito
I travel across your small infinity
dos cuerpos por una sola miel derrotados
two bodies, overcome by one honey.

We drive deliberately as you
always do, never in a hurry,
snow-plowed highways,
looking for Powder Hill Road,
the turn-off to a view of a lake
you remember from a long ago
road trip to Pinkham Notch.

Climbing the one mountain
you are in love with,
you stop every few minutes
to show me
wild orchids growing deep,
lichen coating gray granite
older than we can count,
fresh virgin snow drops, ready,
centuries and centuries of vegetation,
the mystery.

Asking you
what is the lotus fruit?
how are its petals?
why do you smell of lime rind?

How do you cut a mango?
What else can you do with an avocado?

Eating thick, hot French fries from Fritz's,
jalapenos and red peppers
soaked in sour cream,
sitting in the car outside the movie theater,
our fingers, our lips dripping
shall we go in?
half an hour after it has begun,
laughing uncontrollably.

The empty chunks of time
have lost their names, even their minds.
All shimmering thoughts have spilled
like spoiling rubbish on the sidewalk,
the contents still recognizable,
feral dogs rooting through the cold pizza crusts,
melon rinds, soggy yogurt containers
how does sadness hide itself?

AUTHOR INFORMATION (by the author)

I have lived most of my adult life in Greece. I start with this statement because of the unexpectedly vast impact and weight this fact has had on my world views, how I "translate" and survive in my surroundings, and, naturally, what — and even how — I write. The cultural and physical landscapes of New England, where I was born and raised, and those of the Greek/Mediterranean where I have lived for so long, mingle, merge and even coalesce in intriguing and often inexplicable ways in my poetry. I might begin with a winter New Hampshire image, and a thread of Greece will attach itself to the image and pull it in another, surprising direction. I always trust these interventions, these visits; they inevitably create rich narrative tapestries. I believe they are also a large part of *why* I write, not only *what* I write. In the past few years, world political events have also empowered my writing, infusing it with tension, contradiction and sometimes even mystery. Most recently, my writing has centered around the refugee situation in Europe, specifically Turkey and Greece, and my own experiences in the camps and with the immigrants themselves.

I have worked in teaching, writing, editing and counseling; I have also published six books of poetry, one of which, *The Possibility of Red//H Πιθανότητα του Κόκκινο*, published by Hobblebush Books in 2014, is a bi-lingual edition in English and Greek (translated by Irene Theotokatou and Maria Laina). I have won a number of poetry and chapbook contests and prizes and have been nominated for the Pushcart Poetry Anthology twice; my latest book is *Gathering the Soft*, an art/poetry book that circles around the subject of cancer, put out in 2016 by Passager Books. For further information: www.beckysakellariou.com.

CPSIA information can be obtained
at www.ICGtesting.com
Printed in the USA
LVOW12s1439250417
532119LV00002B/416/P